UNWRAPPING THE
MYSTERY OF CHRISTMAS
(Advent Meditations and Prayers for 2018)

THOMAS R. HENDERSHOT

CONTENTS

1
ABOUT ADVENT

Advent is a spiritual journey to Christmas. Thankfully, in an era where many ancient church practices are no longer in vogue, Advent is one tradition that has gained popularity in modern times. The reason is simple. It helps Christians to focus more on what is important during this holiday season. The secular influences during this time are tremendous. The materialism is overwhelming. The parties often forget about Christ and focus solely on human happiness centering on: fun, family, and friends. These are important but are not the reason for the season. Jesus Christ, born of the Virgin, came into the world to save us. That's the reason we celebrate Christmas.

To satisfactorily get to the commemoration of His birth, however, requires some preparation on our part. We live in an age of which often we feel like we don't have the time to prepare adequately for things. We want what we want now. We want it fast. "No waiting" is one of our favorite ads. However, the kingdom of God doesn't work like that. God often spends much time preparing His people before He pours His blessings upon them. We are regularly told to ready ourselves for His activity among us.

Preparation is the theme of the Season of Advent. The birth of God into human flesh was so amazing and significant that it still requires for us to settle our minds and prepare our hearts to receive this tremendous event each year. We gain more from it if we take the time to settle down and contemplate it beforehand. Accepting God and His work in us is a process rather than an event. The better the preparation, the more gratifying and beneficial the experience.

For many, Christmas is an episode rather than a meaningful spiritual experience. Some are busy with their daily activities and preparations for the "big day" and miss the beauty of it. Observing Advent as a season, rather than having Christmas as an event only, helps folks to slow the whole thing down and better think through the meaning of it. The day may still come faster than we want, but it won't be without some meaningful reflection and spiritual contemplation. In fact, I am of the opinion; we should seek to experience a new awareness of the coming of Christ into our world every year. As we prepare our hearts for His holy First Advent, we open up ourselves to receive Him as our Blessed Savior afresh every year, and better ready ourselves for His Second Advent.

Two things are sure in our time. We don't like to wait, and we would rather not have to take time to prepare. Advent Season is an assault on both of these mindsets. In Advent, we wait and prepare for the coming of Jesus represented by Christmas. This alone is a good exercise for us during these times. However, Christians do not wait and prepare only. We wait and prepare with *expectation.*

There are different themes used to celebrate the four weeks of Advent. Christians who observe Advent often use an Advent Wreath and light a different candle each week to symbolize the weekly theme. The light is an emblem of Christ, *The Light of the World*, coming into our dark world as one of us. The highlight of this observance happens on Christmas Eve when lighting the fifth candle, *The Christ Candle*, which is centered between the other four and commemorates His birth.

Not all Christians observe Advent. That's fine. The Bible doesn't command it. I wouldn't tell anyone they must do it. However, any opportunity to get closer to God is a good thing. Any wholesome process which can slow us down and cause us to reflect before celebrating a Holy Day as significant as the birth of Jesus Christ is worth doing in my opinion. It helps to turn it from a holiday to a Holy Day, as it was originally intended to be. Why not set apart some time to intentionally draw closer to God this year and make this Christmas a little less secular, and a little bit more spiritual? I believe you will be glad you did.

For the next twenty-four days we will learn from the scripture and turn our hearts to prayer. I believe God will prepare us for Christmas and cause His Son to be born in each of us in a new awareness of grace as we seek Him. This year we will meditate on some of the mysteries surrounding Jesus, His birth, His Names, and the message of Christmas. Christianity demands a response. Take the time to ask yourself what each aspect of the mystery of Christmas as presented means to you personally. I have also included scripture references for each day at the end of the book for further study for those who might be interested in the passages. "May God grant each one who takes this spiritual journey of unwrapping the mystery of Christmas a renewed awareness of His hope, peace, joy, and love as together we wait expectantly in His presence! Amen."

2
MEDITATIONS ON THE MYSTERY OF CHRISTMAS

FIRST SUNDAY OF ADVENT
December 2, 2018

ZOPHAR'S words

REFLECTION: THE MYSTERY OF GOD
READING: "Can you fathom the mystery of God? Or can you probe the limits of the Almighty?" (Job 11:7)
REVELATION: This verse is not meant to discourage us from searching for truth and understanding. In fact, God calls us to seek Him for both. It is merely saying that we cannot understand the divine things by human methods. Science cannot discover or explain God. Logic and reason fail to experience Him. The human mind cannot comprehend Him. He is too big and too far above us. He is eternal and omniscient. We cannot grasp the mysteries of time and space regarding Him. How can a Being Who is larger than the universe come into the womb of a woman and become the God-

5

man? This question is a mystery of space. How can the Eternal One enter into the dimension of time and live within the constraints of it? This pondering is a mystery of time. Understanding God's mysteries requires revelation. God reveals Himself in many ways, but primarily through His Word and His Spirit. Often, we know a person by their name. In the scripture, sometimes a name revealed much about an individual. God has revealed Himself through His Names, which He has given in His Word. Faith believes God's self-disclosure. Faith is given to us by God's Spirit and gives us the supernatural ability to believe His Word, wherein God has revealed Himself. He sent His Word through His Spirit. He spoke, and His breath carried His Word into time. Jesus is the ultimate revelation of God in human flesh. He is the WORD made flesh, in time and space, implanted within Mary by God's Spirit. **"Can you fathom the mystery of God? Or can you probe the limits of the Almighty?"** Hear and receive the mystery of God today! God has revealed Himself to us by coming to us as a baby in a manger. The Word became flesh.

REQUEST: "Oh God, I open up my heart and mind to the revelation of Your Word and Spirit. You have promised to bless those who seek You and search for You. Help me to see that You have come to us in the Baby Jesus wrapped in swaddling clothes in a manger. Create in me a desire to love You more and know You better during this Advent Season. Amen."

RESPONSE: In what ways does acknowledging the mystery of God challenge my faith?_____

_____

_____

_____

MONDAY – December 3, 2018

REFLECTION: THE MYSTERY OF THE
INCARNATION

READING: "For to us a child is born. To us a son is given; and the government will be on his shoulders. His name will be called Wonderful, Counselor, Mighty God, Everlasting Father, Prince of Peace." (Isaiah 9:6)

REVELATION: Christmas is full of mystery. Let's look now at what is likely the most significant mystery of the Christmas story. Mary conceived Jesus inside of her when the Holy Spirit overshadowed her. Jesus was the WORD that became flesh. That's the incarnation, *"God in the flesh."* Think of it. One moment He is the Eternal Son of God in Heaven. In the next moment, He is as small as a spiritual seed of conception in the realm of humanity, inside of a woman. One moment He is eternal and equal with the Father, and with the Holy Spirit. The next, He is the embryonic child inside of Mary. From that moment of conception through the Holy Spirit, Jesus grew as an embryo taking a human shape inside of Mary over the following months of her gestation period. From the instant of conception, He became uniquely one of us, although He never stopped being the Eternal Son of God. What a mystery!

REQUEST: "Oh Lord God of wonder and mystery, what a gift You gave humanity when Your Son became one of us! Help me to truly believe the mystery that brings me eternal life through Him. In Christ's Name, I ask. Amen."

RESPONSE: How does the mystery of the incarnation change me?_____

_____

_____

7

TUESDAY – December 4, 2018

REFLECTION: THE GREAT MYSTERY

READING: "And without controversy great is the mystery of godliness: God was manifested in the flesh, justified in the Spirit, seen by angels, preached among the Gentiles, believed on in the world, received up in glory."

(1 Timothy 3:16, NKJV)

REVELATION: It is normal that many people struggle with believing that God became a man. It has always been a controversial subject. Paul acknowledged this here in his first letter to Timothy. Questioning this is not just a modern liberal view of the supposed intelligentsia. The fact is, it's not a simple concept for anyone to grasp. It is a great mystery. Christianity is based on divine mysteries, spanning from the creation of the universe to the end-of-time. *Time* itself is a mystery, something we measure but don't understand. The incarnation is one of the mysteries of Christianity. It is a great mystery. Ah, but do not fear! God gives us the faith to believe in the incarnation even though we can never really understand it. The season of Christmas is most meaningful to us when we open our hearts and minds to God's mysterious ways, and when we open our hearts to His revelation to us. This mystery belongs to us today. It is a gift from our Heavenly Father. We can unwrap it through the disclosure of the scripture and the insight of His Spirit. Many of us are a part of the class of Gentiles among whom was declared the message of the incarnation, and who have believed in God manifested in the flesh. We don't fully understand the Great Mystery of the Incarnation, but we believe it! God has given us His Son, robed in our humanity, and we have received His gift. It is a mysterious gift for mere mortals, but one we must accept. As we take this truth into our hearts, God helps us unwrap its precious mysteries. We become those in the world who believe on Him.

REQUEST: "Oh God, open my heart and mind to Your mysterious ways. Help me to believe in the miracle of the incarnation and the blessings it brings to all who trust in You. I receive the One Who was manifested in the flesh to save all who would trust in Him. Help me to trust Jesus more during this Advent Season. I ask this in Your holy Name. Amen."

RESPONSE: In what ways does accepting the truth that Christianity is based on many mysteries challenge my faith? _____

_____
_____
_____
_____

WEDNESDAY – December 5, 2018

REFLECTION: THE MYSTERY OF THE SON

READING: "⁶ For to us a child is born. To us a son is given, and the government will be on his shoulders. His name will be called Wonderful, Counselor, Mighty God, Everlasting Father, Prince of Peace." (Isaiah 9:6)

REVELATION: The incarnation means that God the Son became a human. This joining of the Son with humanity involved all three Persons of the Trinity and Mary. A child was born of God the Father, and a woman, by the work of the Holy Spirit. The Son, Who was fully divine, became fully human (although He didn't cease to be fully divine). He was the Son of God from eternity past. The Son had always been with the Father and the Holy Spirit. He was the eternal Son of God. He became the Son of Man, born of Mary. Joseph was not His earthly father. He was His stepfather. He raised Him as his own, but God was His true Father from eternity and in time. God was His Father, both in eternal spirit and in mortal flesh. God the Father gave His *eternally begotten* Son to be born in time, as the Son of God and the Son of Man. He was the Son of God given by the Father to humanity. He was divinely conceived by God within Mary and became a man. However, He was the Eternal Son of God before this. God gave Him from eternity to become a part of the human race. The Father was His eternal Father and His Father in the conception of Mary. He gave Him from Heaven to humanity in His birth, and for His death.

REQUEST: "Gracious Father, I thank You that You gave us Heaven's best when You gave Your Son to humanity. Help me to give my best to You now and each day, in His Name, Jesus, I ask. Amen."

RESPONSE: How does considering the work of the entire Trinity in the incarnation affect my view of Jesus' birth?_____

_____

_____

_____

THURSDAY – December 6, 2018

REFLECTION: THE MYSTERY OF THE GIFT

READING: "For God so loved the world that He gave His only begotten Son, that whoever believes in Him should not perish but have everlasting life." (John 3:16, NKJV)

REVELATION: Jesus is the *eternally begotten* Son of God. He has always been God's Son. As a man, He was born of Mary around 2 AD. He was then both divine and human. God gave His one, and only eternally begotten Son to enter into time as a human and die for the lost world. He was perfect in His divinity. Jesus was sinless in His humanity. He was the only one who could give His life on earth for sin representing both God and man. The Eternal Son was the most magnificent Christmas Gift a loving God could ever give an undeserving world. Jesus, in His death, offered the very best He could. Father and Son each gave their best for us. Now they give us the Spirit to seal the mystery as we await Heaven and the full outworking of the gift of eternal life in the presence of the Holy Trinity and the angelic hosts.

REQUEST: "It's a mystery, Lord, that You would give Your only begotten Son for me. O' gracious Father, I thank You for giving Your beloved Son for me. Oh, perfect Savior, I thank You for Your obedience to Your Father and for giving Your life for me. I believe! Holy Spirit, please keep me in the love of God. Amen."

RESPONSE: In what ways does beleiving and accepting my salvation as the free gift of God help my faith? _____

_____
_____
_____
_____

FRIDAY – December 7, 2018

REFLECTION: THE MYSTERY OF THE DUAL NATURE

READING: "For there is one God and one mediator between God and mankind, the man Christ Jesus,..."

(1 Timothy 2:5, NIV)

REVELATION: Jesus came to save us. His name means, "Savior." To do this, He had to become one of us. He is our Kinsmen-Redeemer. He became

11

one of us to represent us before God and to die for our sins. He became the mediator between God and man, divinity and humanity. He is both divine and human. He is the one and only go-between Who links together both God and man. He is the bridge. He is the way to the Father. He was born as a baby to become one of us. He died for us that we may become like Him. He is forever one of us. If we receive Him, we are forever one with Him.

REQUEST: "Lord God, what a mystery it is, that the WORD became flesh. He is now in the heavens as one of us. Thank You, Lord, for such a wonderful intercessor and mediator who joins God with humanity. Jesus, the God-man is my Redeemer and Savior. Amen."

RESPONSE: In what ways does realizing that Jesus is fully man and fully God help me to appreciate His sacrafice for me and His understanding of my human challenges in this life?

_____
_____
_____
_____
_____

SATURDAY – December 8, 2018

REFLECTION: THE MYSTERY OF CHRIST IN US

READING: "26The mystery which has been hidden for ages and generations. But now it has been revealed to his saints, 27 to whom God was pleased to make known what are the riches of the glory of this mystery among the Gentiles, which is Christ in you, the hope of glory;.."

(Colossians 1:27-28)

REVELATION: In the incarnation, God came to dwell in humanity. First, God entered into Mary. The

Holy Spirit overshadowed her, and the WORD entered her and joined Himself with human flesh. Christ was born as both human and divine. He is the perfect union of the two natures. After He died for our sins as the Dual-natured Perfect One, He ascended into Heaven and poured out His Spirit upon all flesh. When we receive Him inside of us, He comes in the Person of the Holy Spirit. The indwelling of the Holy Spirit is *Christ in us.* Believing Christians are united with Christ. He lives *in* us. We are humans who are indwelt by God. It is not an incarnation *as* He was, but it is an incarnation *because* He was. We live an incarnational life as those who are *indwelt* by Christ. This mystery produces joy unspeakable! God lives in us. We have received the WORD.

REQUEST: "Dear Lord, You came to dwell among us in Jesus. You joined Yourself to our humanity. Now You come to live inside of us because of Christ. Live in me, precious Spirit. Amen."

RESPONSE: In what ways does acknowledging the mystery of my personal union with Christ enhance my view of the new life I have in God? _____

_____

_____

_____

_____

_____

_____

_____

_____

_____

_____

SECOND SUNDAY OF ADVENT
December 9, 2018

REFLECTION: CHRIST FORMED IN YOU

READING: "My little children, of whom I am again in travail until Christ is formed in you.   (Galatians 4:4)

REVELATION: The *travail* of which Paul speaks of here is his work and prayer. God formed man from the dust. God breathed into the form (body), and it became a living soul, a human being. Adam sinned and lost the *inner* life God had given. Everyone born from Adam comes into the world without this inner spiritual life. There exists both *zoe* and *bios* life, the eternal and the natural. Adam inwardly died when he sinned but continued to live outwardly. Adam lost his internal life source. He lost *zoe.* Receiving Jesus is the only way to get the inner life restored. Jesus is God united with our humanity. Adam was not His father, as he is to all of us. Therefore, Christ was not born in sin as we all are. The spiritual death and darkness of Adam were not passed to Jesus when He became a man. Christ had a spiritual form from the beginning and took a human shape in the incarnation. When we receive Him, He unites us with Himself. We are born anew from connecting with His life. Now let's see a parallel. Christ was born of Mary through conception. In a sense, He was born in us when we believed on Him. We received the seed of the Word of God inside of us, in our spirit. It was a conception of faith. That was the beginning of our faith walk. But we needed to grow. We required formation. Praying for others to believe on Christ unto the new birth is an essential part of the formation of faith in others. Every Christian is called to intercede for the lost. Many hear the Word and do not believe because no one prayed for them. Many do not grow after hearing the Word of God because no one travailed for them. Prayer and the ministry of the Word work together. Christians must pray that the spiritual blindness gets lifted from the lost. When someone receives the Word inside of them, it must take root and formation. That's the goal. Give the greatest gift you have to others this Christmas Season. Share the Word and pray for them. Pray that Christ may be formed in them. Christ inside of a person is our only real hope in this life, and the life to come.

REQUEST: "Father God, continue to transform my inner-man into Christ's image, and help those I name before You now. Lift spiritual blindness, and let Your Word enter into those You have put on my heart today. Bring *zoe* life into dead souls and light into darkness. Advance Your kingdom through my prayers today. In Christ's Name, I ask. Amen."

RESPONSE: In what ways does seeing the profound importance of intercessory prayer challenge you this Advent Season? _____

_____

_____

_____

_____

MONDAY - December 10, 2018

REFLECTION: THE MYSTERY OF HIS NAMES

READING: "For to us a child is born. To us a son is given; and the government will be on his shoulders. His name will be called Wonderful, Counselor, Mighty God, Everlasting Father, Prince of Peace." (Isaiah 9:6)

REVELATION: Names in the Bible and ancient times held great significance. A name revealed

15

one's character and often one's mission in life. This prophecy in Isaiah, some 700 years before Christ's birth, gave the "child to be born" and "son to be given" several significant names. In the manger, wrapped in the swaddling clothes, was more than just a tender newborn human babe. He was God in the flesh. The mystery of Christmas was wrapped up in the names and titles given to Him. Little by little they revealed His mission, purpose, and character. The more we unwrap and uncover, the clearer the gift of Christ to the world becomes. The nature and mission of this Babe were too big and too important to be described with one or two titles, even in this single verse. Increasing our understanding of the vastness of His character and Person comes through discovering the mystery behind His Names. The prophets and writers of the scripture would employ many titles to attempt to describe Christ. This verse is a beautiful example of this. Therefore, throughout the remainder of this book, we will consider many of His names as we seek to unwrap the mystery of Christmas.

REQUEST: "Gracious Father, You have given us Your Son, the One Who is called 'Wonderful, Counselor, Mighty God, Everlasting Father, and the Prince of Peace.' Help me to know Him better throughout this Advent Season as I learn more about the mystery of His Names. Amen."

RESPONSE: How can you personally get to know Jesus better by understanding His divine titles?

_____

_____

_____

_____

_____

TUESDAY – December 11, 2018

REFLECTION: WONDERFUL

READING: "For to us a child is born. To us a son is given; and the government will be on his shoulders. His name will be called Wonderful, Counselor, Mighty God, Everlasting Father, Prince of Peace." (Isaiah 9:6)

REVELATION: His Name is Wonderful. The word "wonderful" has the meaning of, "supernatural or marvelous." His Name is Wonderful because He is supernatural. He was God from the beginning. He has always existed. Although He entered our time as a man, He was from eternity. He is supernatural. He is also marvelous. In the New Testament, the word often used to describe Him was, "Amazing." They "marveled" and were "amazed" at Him. They were amazed at His Person, His Words, and His deeds. Anyone who gets to know Him will be genuinely amazed by Him. If you are not thoroughly amazed at Him, ask Him for a closer relationship right now.

REQUEST: "Father, thank You for sending Your Wonderful Son into the fallen world to save us. Holy Spirit, reveal to me this Wonderful Son of God more and more every day. In Jesus' Name, I ask You, O Lord. Amen."

RESPONSE: In what ways have you experienced Jesus, the Wonderful One? _____

_____

_____

_____

_____

_____

_____

_____

WEDNESDAY – December 12, 2018

REFLECTION: COUNSELOR

READING: "For to us a child is born. To us a son is given; and the government will be on his shoulders. His name will be called Wonderful, Counselor, Mighty God, Everlasting Father, Prince of Peace." (Isaiah 9:6)

REVELATION: It is a mystery to unbelievers as to how Christians receive counsel and comfort from God. They don't understand that we know that Christ is inside of us. The Heavenly Counselor lives in you and me. His Word and Spirit guide us. Some translators combine the first two titles given here as, "Wonderful Counselor." This answers to the kind of counsel He gives His people. It is supernatural and marvelous. It is amazing. To receive sound counsel is a good thing. Sometimes we get into a situation that requires wisdom beyond our limited understanding. Jesus gives us the wisdom we need, when we need it. He offers that kind of counsel to His people. He provides on-time help when we seek for it. But He also gives ongoing counsel as a present benefit of the New Covenant. He comes to dwell within us and joins our spirits with His wisdom. Solomon was regarded as the wisest man in the world. Jesus is greater than Solomon. Christ, the Loving and Wise One is inside of you and me. This special Counselor is not just an on-call counselor. He is an ever-present Counselor.

REQUEST: "Loving Father, I thank You that You have given me Your Son and Your Spirit to lead me and guide me through this life. Teach me to listen to the inner voice that never contradicts Your written Word and always gives good counsel. In Jesus' Name, I pray. Amen."

RESPONSE: In what ways do you know Him as your Counselor? _____

_____

_____

_____

_____

THURSDAY – December 13, 2018

REFLECTION: MIGHTY GOD

READING: "For to us a child is born. To us a son is given; and the government will be on his shoulders. His name will be called Wonderful, Counselor, Mighty God, Everlasting Father, Prince of Peace."   (Isaiah 9:6)

REVELATION: Jesus is the Mighty God. This is a mystery for those who can only see Him as a man, especially as someone whom the Romans shamefully and brutally crucified. But He is also God. He is equal with God. This title means He is the Omnipotent Supreme Ruler of everything. He is the Creator. He holds everything together. The word "mighty" also means, "hero." How fitting this title is for Him. He is the One Who saved us. He did it by leaving Heaven and entering into the womb of Mary. He became one of us so we could become one with Him. He was born to die. That sounds like a real hero to me. He came to live and to die for you and me. Let us not overly exalt mere men: Spoiled sports stars, the filthy Hollywood gang, or the morally depraved pop starts. Jesus is our hero. Let us praise Him!

REQUEST: "Jesus, You are my hero. I turn my heart and affection away from the false heroes of this world and set my affection on You, the lover of my soul, and the Lord, mighty in battle. Amen."

RESPONSE: In what ways do you see Him in your life, and in the world as the Mighty God?

_____

_____

_____

_____

FRIDAY – December 14, 2018

REFLECTION: EVERLASTING FATHER

READING: "For to us a child is born. To us a son is given; and the government will be on his shoulders. His name will be called Wonderful, Counselor, Mighty God, Everlasting Father, Prince of Peace." (Isaiah 9:6)

REVELATION: This title is mysterious for both believers and nonbelievers. However, the scripture here is not saying Jesus is God the Father. The Father is a distinct Person of the Holy Trinity, along with the Son, and the Spirit. The Trinity is, indeed, also a mystery of the Faith of the Church. That is a different subject from this, although we must accept it too to receive the message of Christmas fully. The passage above simply tells us that Jesus is the _source of eternity_. He is the Father of Eternity in the sense that all things come from Him and consist now by Him. All existence is wrapped up in Him. He existed as God before He became a man. He is eternal. Therefore He gives eternal life to all who come to Him in faith. He is the God-man. Although He became a man, He never ceased to be God. He is the Eternal WORD. He spoke the worlds into existence. He is life. He doesn't only have eternal life; He is eternal life. They killed His body only because He laid it down. He also had the power to raise it back up. He is the Father of Eternity Who entered into time to redeem us.

20

REQUEST: "Oh God, I receive eternal life from You today. I know that all life is from You and that eternal life is through Your Son only, the Father of Time and Eternity. I come to You and receive the eternal and unending life You offer me through Christ. I receive Jesus Christ afresh now in this time and expect to be with Him forever. It's in His Name, I pray. Amen."

RESPONSE: How does knowing that He is the Father of all time and eternity strengthen your faith in the present? _____

_____
_____
_____
_____
_____

SATURDAY – December 15, 2018

REFLECTION: PRINCE OF PEACE

READING: "For to us a child is born. To us a son is given, and the government will be on his shoulders. His name will be called Wonderful, Counselor, Mighty God, Everlasting Father, Prince of Peace." (Isaiah 9:6)

REVELATION: This name is mysterious for many to understand in a world plagued with war, strife, and conflict. Nevertheless, He is the Prince of Peace in the midst of a strife-ridden and war-torn world. And peace is one of the great themes of the Advent Season and Christmas time. At the announcement of Christ's birth to the shepherds, the Angelic chorus sang, *"Glory to God in the highest, peace on earth and goodwill to men."* He was called the "Prince of Peace" by the prophet because He is the only One Who can bring lasting peace to us. It has not yet come to us in its completed form. Evil men still fight against God and one another and will until the very end-of-time. The darkness resists the light even now. Jesus brought His peace to earth at His birth. He made peace with God for humanity at His death. Anyone who will receive Him now can have His peace. Many reject His offer to this very day. At the end-of-time, He will smash evil entirely, and His peace will rule directly over all creation. We can have peace with God now by the blood of the cross. We can have the peace of God as will fully commit our lives to Him. We will enjoy everlasting peace when He returns the second time in glory and brings us into the presence of His Father for all eternity.

REQUEST: "Lord God, You sent Your Son to be the Prince of Peace. I bow before Jesus now that He may reign and rule in my heart by His peace. I look forward to the time when He reigns fully for eternity as the Prince of Peace over all creation. Amen."

RESPONSE: How has Jesus brought His peace into your life, and what has resulted from it? _____

_____
_____
_____
_____
_____

THIRD SUNDAY OF ADVENT
December 16, 2018

REFLECTION: SAVIOR
READING: "She shall give birth to a son. You shall call his name Jesus, for it is he who shall save his people from their sins." (Matthew 1:21)
REVELATION: Jesus means, "Yah will save." The end-result of salvation is spending eternity in Heaven rather than in Hell. However, He didn't come only to save us from Hell. He came to save

His people from their sins. Sin destroys us. Sin corrupts us. Sin hurts others. But most importantly, sin is an offense to God and is what caused the death of Jesus. He died to save us from our sin. Sin kills. Death came into the world because of sin. Hell is the second or final death. Therefore, Hell is the ultimate consequence of sin. It is the eternal separation from God. Let us be thankful today that no person needs to go to Hell. God has provided a way to avoid this. Jesus died for our sins. If we trust Him for our salvation, we are no longer condemned to an eternity in Hell.

REQUEST: "Blessed Savior, I come to You today acknowledging my sin and receiving Your forgiveness and cleansing. It is a great mystery to me that You could put my sin on Your Son and give me His righteousness. Give me faith to believe this wonderful truth and assurance that my name is written down in Your Book of Life. Because of Jesus, I believe You will take me to Heaven when I die. As I continue to live on this earth, help me to live righteously before You and remember that my sin nailed Jesus to the cross. In His precious Name, I pray. Amen."

RESPONSE: How do you know Him as your Savior, and with whom in your life might Christ want you to share your story? _____

_____

_____

_____

_____

_____

_____

_____

_____

MONDAY – December 17, 2018

REFLECTION: IMMANUEL

READING: "Therefore the Lord himself will give you a sign. Behold, the virgin will conceive, and bear a son, and shall call his name Immanuel." (Isaiah 7:14)

REVELATION: Jesus is the sign on earth of God's great salvation. God has provided the way to Heaven for us through His Son. Immanuel means, "God with us." This name shocked those who heard it. They could not fathom the mystery of the Omnipotent God dwelling in human form. When God the Son became a human, it was forever. It was not temporary. It was not just for His life and ministry. It was not only for His death on the cross. It was forever. He arose from the dead and ascended into Heaven as the God-man. Spirit and flesh are forever united in the Lord Jesus Christ. He sits at the right hand of God now as the God-man. We shall see Him in Heaven as the God-man. He is forever the bridge between divinity and humanity. He is the way to the Father. He is the only way to Heaven.

REQUEST: "Father in Heaven, I come to You now in the Name of Jesus and because of Him. I thank You today for such a mediator and intercessor. I receive Your gift of salvation through Jesus Christ, Your Son, my Savior, and Lord. Amen."

RESPONSE: In what ways has God showed you He is with you? _____

_____

_____

_____

_____

_____

_____

_____

TUESDAY – December 18, 2018

REFLECTION: THE WORD OF GOD

READING: "¹In the beginning was the Word, and the Word was with God, and the Word was God... ¹⁴ And the Word became flesh and dwelt among us, and we have seen his glory, glory as of the only Son from the Father, full of grace and truth.Word became flesh, and lived among us. We saw his glory, such glory as of the one and only Son of the Father, full of grace and truth."   (John 1:1, 14, ESV)

REVELATION: The mystery of the WORD becoming flesh is one of the chief mysteries of the Christian Faith. Before Jesus was born of Mary, He was the WORD. He did not have a beginning. He is eternal. He has always existed with the Father and the Holy Spirit. Even before time, He was face-to-face in intimate communion with the Father and the Holy Spirit. That is the meaning of the phrase *"with God"* in the original language. The WORD (Gr. Logos) entered into the womb of Mary as the Holy Spirit overshadowed her. We cannot comprehend this. It is a mystery. The flesh He received from His natural mother became *the tent* in which He lived for 33 years on earth. That is the meaning of *"dwelt among us"* in the Greek. Mary gave Him a temporary house to live in for His natural life here. At the resurrection, God took the crucified broken body of Jesus and made it eternal, as He promises to do for us also on the Last Day. The resurrection of the body is another profound mystery of our Faith. We will rise again from the grave because He arose. He arose because He was crucified. He was able to be crucified because He became flesh. Glory to God! His name is the WORD of GOD. The WORD became flesh and dwelt among us. The WORD lives in those who receive Him even now. The WORD

25

resides in the human bodies of believers, and by the Spirit, will quicken our bodies at the resurrection of the dead.

REQUEST: "Father God, I thank You that the WORD became flesh and lived and died for me. I believe this and receive Him. I believe He will come again, raise the dead, and transform the living believers to be with Him. He gives us new life now as we believe in Him and will raise our bodies on the Last Day. Death is the last enemy, and my Lord will destroy it. I trust Your promise that He will come again to earth as the Judge and Warrior wearing a vesture dipped in blood and will overcome evil permanently. He is the WORD of God with a two-edged sword in His mouth. Make me ready to ride on a white horse with Him. Amen."

RESPONSE: In what ways do you show God that you value His Word? _____

_____

_____

_____

_____

_____

_____

WEDNESDAY – December 19, 2018

REFLECTION: THE LAMB OF GOD

READING: "The next day he saw Jesus coming toward him, and said, "Behold, the Lamb of God, who takes away the sin of the world!" (John 1:29, ESV)

REVELATION: The mystery of the Passover Lamb is better understood as we realize that Jesus came to die vicariously as the Lamb of God for the sin of the world. The blood of a flawless Passover Lamb had to be applied to the doorposts of the homes by those who believed. The lamb had to die, and the blood had to be applied. The death angel did not hold back (pass over) in executing judgment on those who did not apply the blood of the lamb. When we believe on Christ, we place our trust in His blood. By faith, we apply His blood. Had He never become a man, He would have had no blood to shed. Again, the birth of Christ as the Son of Mary was crucial. Had He had a man as His father, His blood would not have been pure. Again, the truth of miraculous conception by the Holy Spirit is critical. He died as the perfect Lamb of God, and we are spared eternal death by receiving Him and trusting in the efficaciousness of His blood poured out for us and applied to our hearts by faith.

REQUEST: "My Lord and God, You came to earth to die. You came to give Your life for me. How can I thank You for this by doing anything less than living my life for You? Grant me the grace I need to live for You, loving Jesus. Amen."

RESPONSE: Have you personally acknowledged Christ's death as the Lamb of God for you, and how has this changed you? _____

_____

_____

_____

_____

THURSDAY – December 20, 2018

REFLECTION: THE LION OF JUDAH

READING: "[1] I saw, in the right hand of him who sat on the throne, a book written inside and outside, sealed shut with seven seals. [2] I saw a mighty angel proclaiming with a loud voice, "Who is worthy to open the book, and to break its seals?" [3] No one in heaven above, or on the earth, or under the earth, was able to open the book, or to look in it. ⁴ And I wept much, because no one was found worthy to open the book, or to look in it. ⁵ One of the elders said to me, "Don't weep. Behold, the Lion who is of the tribe of Judah, the Root of David, has overcome; he who opens the book and its seven seals." ⁶ I saw in the middle of the throne and of the four living creatures, and in the middle of the elders, a Lamb standing, as though it had been slain, having seven horns, and seven eyes, which are the seven Spirits of God, sent out into all the earth. ⁷ Then he came, and he took it out of the right hand of him who sat on the throne."   (Revelation 5:1-7)

REVELATION: Today we shall consider the mysterious paradox of a heavenly vision of duality, the Lion Who is a slain Lamb. Jesus has a dual nature. He is fully God and fully human. He is the Son of God and the Son of Man. In His humanity, He is also both the Lion and the Lamb. Both of these dynamic characteristics of His humanity are displayed here. The title "Lion of Judah" emphasizes the humanness of Jesus showing that He is connected *forever* with humanity. But He is also divine. Here, the Lion is in Heaven and is of the tribe of Judah, the root of David. Even in Heaven, He is forever linked with humanity. He never stopped being human. Jesus ascended into Heaven as the God-man. The Old Testament Passover lamb was temporary. Although He was fully human, the Lamb of God Who took away the sin of the world is eternal. This Lion of Judah Who is a slain Lamb is everlasting as the eternal God-man. His work of redemption will continue forever. He triumphed as a Lion over the devil, the flesh, and the world. He is as strong as a lion because He was willing to be slain as a lamb. He demonstrated His strength in human weakness, as a lamb slain. The great victorious Lion is now in Heaven as the Lord of all. The Lamb's victory is ours to share as we bow before Him and declare, "Thou art worthy." "The Lion of the tribe of Judah has overcome."

REQUEST: "You are worthy, O Lord. You have redeemed the entire universe by Your precious blood. Your death dealt a death blow to death. Death reigned over humanity since Adam. Now life is freely given to any who will call upon Your Name. You grew from the Babe in the manger to the Lion of the tribe of Judah. I bow my head in worship to You now. Amen."

RESPONSE: How does acknowledging the victory of Christ through His suffering help you better understand your sufferings? _____

_____

_____

_____

_____

_____

FRIDAY – December 21, 2018

REFLECTION: THE MESSIAH

READING: "Today in the town of David a Savior has been born to you; he is the Messiah, the Lord. " (Luke 2:11, NIV)

REVELATION: Throughout the Old Testament the people of God longed for the coming of the Messiah. He was the "Anointed One" Who would someday deliver Israel. His full work and the method in which He would carry out God's plan was a mystery to the people and leaders. Some of the prophets got a glimpse of it from time to time. The New Testament word, "Christ" means the same thing as the Old Testament "Messiah." Jesus is God's "Anointed One." That's what *Messiah* and *Christ* both mean.

He was chosen from before time to do everything He did. Jesus was the only One Who could do these things. He had to be born as a man to do them. This is why we celebrate Christmas, His birth. Had He never become as a man, we could never have received salvation. That's how vital Christmas is. The "Anointed One" went about doing good and healing those whom the devil had oppressed. We must come to Jesus and recognize that He is the Christ, the Anointed One, the One Who defeated sin and Satan on our behalf, to receive His blessings. We must accept Him to receive the new life He offers. Seeing and understanding the mystery of Christ can happen to us only by receiving a revelation from God.

REQUEST: "Father God, You sent Your Son to be Lord and Christ among us. He is the "Anointed One." I bow my knee unto Him and accept Him as my Savior and Lord. Help me to lead others to receive Him. In Jesus' Name, I pray. Amen."

RESPONSE: In what ways has receiving the Messiah changed your life, and how have you shared this with others? _____

_____

_____

_____

_____

_____

_____

_____

_____

_____

_____

_____

_____

SATURDAY – December 22, 2018

REFLECTION: THE ALPHA AND OMEGA

READING: "⁷ Behold, He is coming with clouds, and every eye will see Him, even they who pierced Him. And all the tribes of the earth will mourn because of Him. Even so, Amen. ⁸ "I am the Alpha and the Omega, *the* Beginning and *the* End," says the Lord, "who is and who was and who is to come, the Almighty." (Revelation 1:7-8, NKJV)

REVELATION: How can one person be both the beginning and the end? It's a mystery! Let's consider it for a moment. Everything begins and ends with Him. He created all things and will bring everything to conclusion. He is Alpha and Omega. These are the first and last letters of the Greek alphabet. For us, it would be the *A* and *Z*. Everything in God's purposes starts and ends with Him. Earlier we looked at the passages that call Jesus, "The WORD." The *A* to the *Z* is all of the letters that make up the WORD. Everything is summed up in Jesus. He is the Person speaking in this text. He tells John He is the One, *"Who is, and Who was, and Who is to come."* That means He is, "the past, the present, and the future." He is the "Timeless One" Who entered into time to be born as one of us. How can one who is without beginning or ending enter into time? No wonder He ends His set of self-descriptive titles here as, "The Almighty." Dear reader, this passage reveals to us more of the mystery of Christmas. When we trust Him as our Savior, He becomes the "Author" and "Finisher" of our faith. That means He's the *"A* to *Z"* of your faith. It starts, is kept, and finishes with Him. "May we put our complete trust in Him today!"

REQUEST: "Almighty God, You are the First and the Last, the Beginning and the End, The Alpha and

31

Omega. However, You came to be one of us to save us. Although I cannot comprehend these mysteries, let my faith rest solely in You, I ask. Amen."

RESPONSE: In what ways can you begin trusting the Alpha and Omega more in your daily life? _____

_____

_____

_____

_____

_____

FOURTH SUNDAY OF ADVENT
December 23, 2018

REFLECTION: THE BRIGHT MORNING STAR

READING: "I, Jesus, have sent my angel to give you this testimony for the churches. I am the Root and the Offspring of David, and the bright Morning Star."

(Revelation 22:16, NIV)

REVELATION: The star is a symbol of God bringing His light into our dark world. The wise men followed the mysterious star because of the special insight they had received from God about the birth of Christ. They were seeking out the mystery of Christmas. The mysterious star stood over the house where Jesus was. When they saw it, they rejoiced with exceeding great joy and came into the house and fell before Jesus and worshipped Him. The star in the sky was a symbol of the reality of the *Bright Morning Star* Who was in the manger. The term, "Morning Star" is a phrase used for the sun. The birth of the baby Jesus was the Light coming into the world in a new and profound way. This Light would drive out the darkness that had held man in bondage since the fall of Adam and Eve in the Garden of Eden. Jesus is the very radiance of God

32

shining into the earth. His birth was Light born into darkness. It is *bright* because of the darkness of sin. His light, which the darkness could not overcome, still shines into all men's hearts. Many resist it. Have you allowed the *Sun* of God to shine upon you? To receive His radiance upon us is the only hope any of us have in this dark world.

REQUEST: "God of Light, You spoke into the darkness in the first creation. You sent the Sun of Righteousness into our world with healing in His rays. You shine on us giving us life. Shine on me today. Save me and heal me through the rays of the *Sun* of God. Amen."

RESPONSE: In what ways can you worship Christ this year as the Bright and Morning Star of your life?

_____

_____

_____

_____

_____

_____

_____

MONDAY, CHRISTMAS EVE
December 24, 2018

REFLECTION: THE LORD OF LORDS AND KING OF KINGS

READING: "¹²The ten horns you saw are ten kings who have not yet received a kingdom, but who for one hour will receive authority as kings along with the beast. ¹³ They have one purpose and will give their power and authority to the beast. ¹⁴ They will wage war against the Lamb, but the Lamb will triumph over them because he is Lord of lords and King of kings—and with him will be his called, chosen and faithful followers." (Revelation 17:12-14, NIV)

REVELATION: In a grand Christmas mystery, Jesus was born a king. I realize He wasn't born in a palace. I know His parents weren't wealthy. I understand He didn't have an earthly throne. But make no mistake about it, He was born the King of all. The verse above shows the final consummation of His Kingship. Jesus was the newborn King of Israel. He was also born King of the earth, but His kingdom was even more magnificent than this planet. It was more vast than an earthly kingdom in its sphere, time, and dimension. He still welcomes into His Kingdom all who trust Him for salvation. Even so, He rules over all, including those who resist Him and rebel against God. His followers are born from above, translated into His Kingdom of Light, and given to share in His inheritance. The Lord Jesus Christ, the God-man, has ridden victoriously through history and at the end will exercise a final show of His triumph over all evil. The little baby, small enough to fit into the crib, was larger than the world into which He was born. He was not just born to be King of the Jews. He was born to be King and Ruler of the entire universe.

REQUEST: "My Lord and my King, I bow before You now and worship You. I cannot begin to comprehend how great and wonderful You are. Give me faith to know You and trust You, My Lord, my God, and my King. Amen."

RESPONSE: In what ways does acknowledging Christ as Lord of lords, and King of kings help you better face the future? _____

_____

_____

_____

_____

TUESDAY, CHRISTMAS DAY
December 25, 2018

REFLECTION: THE AMEN

READING: "And to the angel of the church of the Laodiceans write, 'These things says the Amen, the Faithful and True Witness, the Beginning of the creation of God."

(Revelation 3:14, NKJV)

REVELATION: It's Christmas Day. Praise God! Perhaps one of the greatest mysteries of Christmas is found in how it seems always to bring a unique feeling each year we celebrate it. This truth must be more than just the family and friends we enjoy. I believe it is because Christ is ever new as we spend more and more time getting to know Him. He is the "Amen." "Amen" is the declaration of God that says, "It shall be done." Because of Jesus, "It is done." Jesus is that WORD of God that says, "It is finished." Every promise of God comes to us through Him. Jesus, the "Amen," is the God of truth speaking to us as a Man. The "Amen" is the *assurance* of all of the promises of God. Christmas means, "Jesus has come to be the "Amen" to what God has promised humanity." No more striving to find God or receive His blessings is needed. We are called to say, "Yes" to the "Amen."

REQUEST: "Lord God of past, present, and the future. You have said, "Amen" in Christ. I thank You for Christmas, and I say, "Yes" to the "Amen." Help me to worship today and to share the hope I have in You with others. In Jesus' name. Amen."

RESPONSE: In what ways do you need to hear the "Amen" of God spoken in your life? How are you willing to open your ears to hear Him speak afresh into your heart this year? _____

SCRIPTURE REFERENCES:

December 2, 2018: Psalm 33:6, Jeremiah 33:3, John 1:1, 1 Corinthians 2:7-16, Hebrews 11:6.

December 3, 2018: Isaiah 7:14, Matthew 1:23, Luke 1:31-38, John 1:1-3, 14.

December 4, 2018: Luke 1:34, John 1:12, 1 Corinthians 2: 8, 1 Peter 1:20, 1 john 1:2, 3:16, Hebrews 2:14.

December 5, 2018: Genesis 1:26, John 17:5, Colossians 1:15-17, 2:2, Hebrews 1:5-12.

December 6, 2018: Luke 11:13, Acts 2:33, John 15:13, 26, 16:12-15, Romans 5:5, 8-9, Ephesians 1:13.

December 7, 2018: Leviticus 25:27, 48, Ruth 4:6-11, John 14:1-6, 2 Corinthians 5:21, Revelation 5:9.

December 8, 2018: 1 Corinthians 6:17, 12:13, 1 John 4:4.

December 9, 2018. Genesis 2:7, Job 33:6, Psalm 139:13, Isaiah 44:2, Jeremiah 1:5, Acts 6:4, 1 Timothy 2:1-4, 2 Corinthians 4:3-4, Philippians 2:6-7, Colossians 1:27, James 1:21, 1 Peter 1:22-25.
Note: The Christmas Hymn, *"O Little Town of Bethlehem"* written in 1835 by Phillips Brooks, D.D., made a similar collation.

December 10, 2018: Genesis 17:5, 32:27-28, Matthew 1:21.

December 11, 2018: Matthew 9:8.

December 12, 2018: Isaiah 11:1-2, Luke 11:31, John 16:13-15, 1 Corinthians 2:30.

December 13, 2018: John 1:3, Philippians 2:5, Colossians 1:16-17.

December 14, 2018: Genesis 1:1-3, John 1:1-5, 11-12, 10:18, 14:6, 17:5, Colossians 1:17, Hebrews 1:1-12, 11:3.

December 15, 2018: Numbers 6:22-23, Isaiah 9:7, 11:6, 26:3, Luke 2:14, Romans 5:1, Philippians 4:6-910, Colossians 3:15, Hebrews 9:28, Revelation 19:11-16.

December 16, 2018: Genesis 3:3, John 10:10, Romans 6:23, 8:1, 1 John 1:8-10, Revelation 20:14-15.

December 17, 2018: Matthew 1:23, John 14:6-11, Acts 2:33, 4:12, Colossians 2:9, 1 Timothy 2:5, Hebrews 7:25.

December 18, 2018: Luke 1:35, John 17:3, 1 Corinthians 6:19-20, 15:26, 50-55, 2 Corinthians 6:16-17, 1 Thessalonians 4:13-18, 1 John 1:1-2, Revelation 19:13.

December 19, 2018: Genesis 4:2-4, 22:13-14, Exodus 12:21-23, Acts 20:28, 1 Corinthians 5:7, 1 Peter 1:18-19, Revelation 1:5, 5:9-13, 12:11.

December 20, 2018: Genesis 49:9-10, Isaiah 11:1, 53:7.

December 21, 2018: Isaiah 53:1-5, Psalm 22, Matthew 2:4-6, 16:13-18, Luke 4:17-18, Acts 2:36, 10:38, 1 Corinthians 2:8-10, Revelation 13:8-9.

December 22, 2018: Psalm 90:2, Michah 5:2, John 8:56-58, Ephesians 1:4-10, Hebrews 1:1-2, 12:1-2.

December 23, 2018: Genesis 1:1-3, Psalm 19:4-6, Malachi 4:2, Matthew 2:1-11, 2 Peter 1:19.

December 24, 2018: Psalm 2, 29. John 3:1-5, 1 Corinthians 6:9-11, Colossians 1:12-13.

December 25, 2018: John 1:1-3, 2 Corinthians 1:20, Hebrews 1:1-2.

ABOUT THE AUTHOR

Rev. Tom Hendershot has written several books on Bible topics to help those to whom he has served as a Pastor and Teacher in the Body of Christ. Rev. Hendershot is affiliated as an ordained minister with the Evangelical Association of Reformed and Congregational Christian Churches (EA) and serves as a member of the National Board of Directors, and as the State Representative of Kentucky and Southern Indiana. Tom and his wife, Angela, have served together in ministry around the world. They minister presently in pastoral ministry at Jerusalem Church in New Philadelphia, Ohio (www.jcnp21.com).

You can obtain other books by this author from:

Create Space: www.createspace.com
Amazon: www.amazon.com
Barnes and Noble: www.barnesandnoble.com
Alibris: www.alibris.com
Evangelical Association:
www.evangelicalassociation.org

Insights for Daily Living Series
(Devotional Series)
Worshipping, Working, and Waiting (1 Thessalonians)
Worthy of the Kingdom (2 Thessalonians)
God's Mysteries Revealed (Ephesians)

Secrets of the Blessed Life Series
The Blessing in the Valley (Psalm 84)
Covenant Confidence (Psalm 25)
The Shamar Blessing (Psalm 121)
Samach (Psalm 16)

Evangelical Essentials (Basic Lessons)
Book One: Four Foundation Stones
Book Two: Resurrection and Judgment
Book Three: Practical Christian Living

Evangelical Essentials Series

Book One: The Name and Nature of God
Book Two: Holy Baptism
Book Three: Holy Communion
Book Four: Essential Eschatology

Pastoral Perspectives Series

First Corinthians, Book One: Spiritual Wisdom for the
Church (ch. 1-3)
Book Two: Wisdom in Practical
Matters (ch. 4-7)
First & Second Thessalonians

General Subjects

Doors
Possessing the Land
Ministry to the Sick
Saints in Strange Situations
Guarding Your Heart and Mind
Psalms, Hymns, and Spiritual Songs
Christ is Our Passover Lamb
Celebrating Pentecost
Clarifying Christianity
Prayer Made Easy
Strongholds
Conscience
Under Pressure

Other Devotionals

Unwrapping the
Mystery of Christmas: Advent Meditations and Prayers
(2018 Season)

40 Days with
Christ in the Desert: A Lenten Devotional

Email for Tom Hendershot: Hendetr@yahoo.com

Made in the USA
Columbia, SC
13 November 2018